JOKEY BOOK AND THE JOKEY BOOK LOGO
© 2023 GLASDEK LTD ALL RIGHTS
RESERVED

FOR MY BEST FRIEND

Why can't Cinderella play football?

She keeps running away from the ball!

What's the angriest part of a football pitch?

The CROSS-bar

How do you end a football match?

With the letter H

QUICK QUIZ

CAN YOU NAME THE TWO NATIONS WHO HAVE WON THE WORLD CUP, BUT ONLY WON IT ONCE?

5 = BRAZIL
4 = ITALY AND GERMANY
3 = ARGENTINA
2 = FRANCE AND URUGUAY
1 = _____ AND _____ ?

WHO IS FASTER: MBAPPE OR A CHEETAH?

The fastest speed that French front-man, Kylian Mbappe has ever recorded was 38 km/h (or 23.6 MPH for us here in the UK), during a Ligue 1 match for PSG against his former club, AS Monaco.

The fastest ever speed recorded for a Cheetah, on the other hand, was almost THREE TIMES as fast. Whilst resident of the Cincinatti zoo in Ohio, USA, Sarah (also known as Sahara) was recorded as running a distance of 100m in just 5.95 seconds, (for context, Usain Bolt's human world record is 9.59 seconds), which is 98 km/h (or 61 MPH). Sorry Mbappe fans. He just can't compete.

WINNER: CHEETAH

MBAPPEEEEE!!

What kind of coffee would you drink if you were a top French striker?

An M-frappe!

What do the French wear when they are babies?

An M-Nappy

Why do PSG players not get loud on the team bus?

Because they will get an M-slap-e!

Who is the biggest clown in the French national team?

SILLY-an Mbappe

Which striker is the worst at making a cup of tea for his team-mates

SPILL-ian Mbappe

Which French Superstar has the best technique?

SKILL-ian Mbappe

Who is the most dangerous striker in world football?

KILL-ian Mbappe

Who is the smallest striker in the world?

Kyli-ANT Mbappe

What do you call a French footballer in a Drake video?

Kylian M-RAP-E

Who is the coolest player at PSG?

CHILL-ian Mbappe

How did the France national team feel when they won the world cup in 2018?

Very M-HAPPY!

Who does barbie love most in football?

Kylian KEN-bappe

FRANCE: la FRANCE
Ligue 1

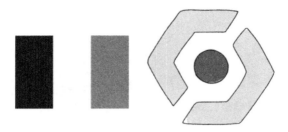

In France, where do players who want to cheat, learn how to dive?

At the I FELL Tower

Who are the most bad-tempered team in Ligue 1?

AS MOAN-aco

Which French team are on another planet?

MARS-eille

Which French team does your brother's daughter play for?

Nice!

TIP: Pronounce it the French way, not the English way

Which team in Ligue 1 sound like they should be playing in the Bundesliga?

Paris Saint-GERMAN

PLAYING FOR THE WRONG COUNTRY XI

WHO

Ben **CHILE**-well
England

Antoine **GREECE**-man
France

DEN-MARKus Rashford
England

Kalidou Kouli-**BALI**
Senegal

Erling **HOLLAND**
Norway

Marc-André Ter-**SWEDEN**
Germany

Frenkie De **HONG-KONG**
Holland

David **AL(a)BA-NIA**
Austria

PHIL-LIPPINES Foden
England

Aaron **TAIWAN**-Bissaka
England

BRAZILIAN Mbappe
France

WINS? CHRISTMAS XI

HOLLY Watkins
Aston Villa

ADVENT Alexander-Arnold
Liverpool

SAN(TA)-dro Tonali
Newcastle

Kim **MIN(CE PIE)-Jae**
Bayern Munich

Harry Candy-**KANE**
Bayern Munich

BETH-lehem Mead
Arsenal Women

Édouard **THREE WISE MEN**-dy
Al-Ahli

SNOW Willock
Newcastle

THE ANGEL GABRIEL Magalhães
Arsenal

♪ Gabriel **JESUS** Christ our saaaaviour was born on Christmas Day ♪
Arsenal

Dayot Upameca**NO-EL**
Bayern Munich

WHO IS TALLER: CROUCH OR A GIRAFFE?

Although way above average height for a human, standing at 6ft7in; king of the robot Peter Crouch is tiny compared to George – who was a resident at Chester Zoo way back in 1959.

George was the tallest giraffe ever recorded, he stood at over 20 feet tall, (the size of two goals stacked on top of each other!) and was apparently unstoppable when coming in at the back post off a corner!

CROUCH   GEORGE

WINNER: GIRAFFE

QUICK QUIZ

CAN YOU NAME THE ONLY TWO NATIONS WHO HAVE PLAYED EACH OTHER IN BOTH A WORLD CUP FINAL, AND A EUROPEAN CHAMPIONSHIPS FINAL?

_____ AND _____

ITALY: ITALIA
SERIE A

Which club in Serie A are the coldest?

Winter Milan!

What's the first thing they teach you at the Italian football academy?

How to pasta ball

> TIP: Deliver this joke in an Italian accent for maximum effect!

Which Serie A team are the sleepiest?

NAP-oli

Why do Italian substitutes get so upset?

They want to get a pizza the action

Why are Italian football fans always in Lockdown?

Because of CO-ROMA virus

ANIMAL KINGDOM

What trophy do monkeys play for?

The CHIMP-ions league

Why do sheep find it hard to score goals?

They keep hitting the BAAAA!

What happens to the worst team in the crocodile league?

They get rele-GATOR-ed

What award does the best player in the tiger league get?

The Ballon ROAR!

What is an eagle's best position?

Winger!

Why can't the team of zebras get the ball into their opponent's half?

They're too scared to go past the half-way Lion

What team do canines support?

Wolves!

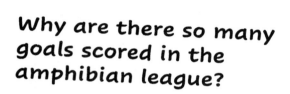

Why are there so many goals scored in the amphibian league?

They have no trouble hitting the back of the NEWT

Why are Lions hard to beat at football?

Because they ROAR so many goals

BREAKING NEWS!!

The winners of the animal league have launched a bid to sign Jamie Vardy from Leicester...

...their manager says they need a striker who is a fox in the box!!

What team do dog owners support?

Leeds

Why do chickens get so many red and yellow cards?

Because they're always FOWL-ing

Who is a canine's favourite left-back?

Destiny U-**DOGGY** (Spurs)

Who scores the most goals in the primate league?

The GOAL-rilla

How does a lion know when he is offside?

When the LIONS-man puts his flag up

WHO CAN JUMP HIGHER: RONALDO OR A FLEA?

Amazingly, Ronaldo's highest ever recorded jump was NOT that header for Juventus against Sampdoria in the 19/20 season. He actually recorded a height of 2.93meters whilst playing for Real Madrid against Manchester United in a 12/13 season Champions League tie. Subtracting his height of 1.87metres, this means that Ronaldo's feet were 1.16metres (3ft9in) off the ground!

Although fleas don't have wings, they can catapult themselves skywards up to 100 times their own body length! Unfortunately though, because they are so small, this only gets them to around 2 feet off the ground, which is just over half of Ronaldo's highest jump. Still pretty impressive though.

WINNER: RONALDO

Insert the name of your rivals here....

Take the following jokes and insert the name of your rival club where prompted, to give them a good roasting...!

What's the difference between _(insert name of your rivals here)_ and a teabag?

A teabag stays in the cup longer!

TIP: Works well if your rivals are: Spurs, Everton, Man United

TIP: Works well if your rivals are: Arsenal, Man City, Chelsea

Why is _(insert name of your rivals here)_'s stadium so hot?

They don't have enough fans

What does a *(insert name of your rivals here)* **fan do when their team wins the league?**

Gets up and turns off their X-BOX!

TIP: Works well if your rivals are: anyone other than Man City!

What is the difference between *(insert name of your rivals here)* **and a toothpick?**

A toothpick's got two points

TIP: Works well if your rivals only get a draw (1 point) against a rubbish team

What is the difference between *(insert name of your rivals here)* **and a big bucket of smelly farts?**

The bucket!

One day, a *(insert name of your rivals here)* **fan is walking through the park when he sees two** *(insert name of your rivals here)* **season tickets nailed to a tree –**

– so, he has a quick look around, checks that no one is looking, and then... steals the nails.

TIP: Works well if your rivals are: Arsenal

TIP: Works well if your rivals are: West Ham, Man United

Why are *(insert name of your rivals here)* **just like a three-pin plug?**

They're both useless in Europe

How do pirates know when it's a penalty?

They check VA-aaaaaaaargh!

BREAKING NEWS!!

Jurgen Klopp has told his Liverpool players that every time they play an FA cup tie they should always try and draw the match...

...he says it is the only way they can guarantee to get a replay!

ZLATAAAAN!!

FACT: When Zlatan is late for training, the manager gives fines to the other players for being too early

FACT: Zlatan tells VAR whether he is offside or not

FACT: When Zlatan does push ups, he is not pushing himself up, he is pushing the planet down

ZLATAAAAN!!

FACT: If Zlatan gets a red card, the referee is the one who leaves the pitch

FACT: When Zlatan scores, it counts as two goals

FACT: In training, Zlatan practises his free kicks with a bowling ball

FACT: When Zlatan gets a yellow card, the player he fouled has to miss the next match

FACT: Zlatan laces up his football boots with his feet

ZLATAAAAN!!

FACT: Zlatan's left foot is also his right foot; Everything about Zlatan is right

FACT: Zlatan once bicycle kicked a horse on the chin, that's how giraffes were created!

FACT: When Zlatan went to school, the teachers raised their hand if they wanted to talk to him

FACT: When Zlatan plays at your stadium, your team is the away team

How badly does Deadpool beat his enemies?

He absolutely Wrecks 'em...

What happens to a team's worst defenders?

They get LEFT-BACK in the dressing room!

What is the difference between Luton Town and Manchester United? ← SICK BURN

One of these teams weren't a bad side back in the day, but they're not good enough for the premiership anymore, they don't have enough fans to fill their stadium and they'll probably get relegated...

...and the other team is Luton...

What football stadium would you go to, to sunbathe?

TANfield...
(Liverpool)

...And where would you never get a tan, because its freezing?

Cold Trafford
(Manchester United)

What is a dog's favourite stadium?

Goodison BARK
(Everton)

What stadium do Italians most want to visit when they come to England?

The SPAGHETTI-had
(Manchester City)

Which Spanish stadium is the hottest?

The BURN-abeu
(Real Madrid)

In which stadium do witches brew their potions?

The Vicente CAULDRON
(Atletico Madrid)

Which Italian stadium does your Mum's Mum want to go to?

The NAN Siro
AC Milan / Inter Milan

Where do you not want to go, in case you get conned?

SCAM-ford bridge
Chelsea

QUICK QUIZ

CAN YOU NAME THE ONLY TWO NATIONS WHO HAVE WON BOTH THE MEN'S AND WOMEN'S WORLD CUPS?

_____ AND _____

WHO IS A BETTER DRIBBLER: MESSI OR A BABY?

Newborn babies don't have full control yet, over the muscles that control swallowing, which is why they expel so much dribble, and on average they'll produce about a litre a day from age 3months to age 15 months (so a year).

Lionel Messi's career dribbling stats show that he has successfully completed an average of 4.56 dribbles per game, putting him firmly in number one over the length of his career. Messi's average carry of the ball when completing dribbles is 13.4 metres, and at the time I am writing this he has played 900 career matches, meaning that he has successfully dribbled a total of 12,060 meters in his career (7½ miles!)

The baby's 365 litres of dribble, when converted into cubic centimetres is equivalent to 3,650 metres (2¼ miles).

Quite a lot of maths there, well done if you kept up with it! The final result is that Lionel Messi is over three times a better dribbler than an average baby!

WINNER: MESSI

FINEST FOODS

What is a Birmingham fan's most hated flavour of ice cream?

Aston Vanilla

Which team makes the best food?

CHEF-ield United

When do Indian football fans get most excited?

When their team gets a KORMA

Which player needs to go on a diet..?

Ansu FATI
(Barcelona / Brighton)

...and which player definitely doesn't?

Skinny Jr
(Real Madrid)

Which team goes well in a sandwich?

West HAM United

Who makes the post-match meal for the linesmen?

The CHEF-eree

FINEST FOODS

How does a kebab shop owner score his goals?

He CHIPS the keeper

Who is the healthiest eater in football?

Mo Salad...

...And who is the UN-healthiest?

Robert Lewan-DONUT-ski

Who is the freshest footballer in the premiership?

Heung-MINT Son

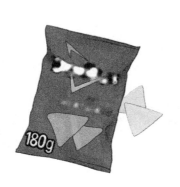

What do you get if you cross a Man United playmaker with a packet of Doritos?

CRISPS-tian Eriksen

What do you get if you cross an Arsenal winger with a kid's birthday party?

Gabriel Marti-JELLY

SPAIN: ESPAGÑA
La Liga

QUESTION: If there are two teams in Madrid, and one is called Real...

...shouldn't Atletico really be called <u>Fake Madrid</u>???

What team do Spanish car salesman support?

CAR SELL-ona

What's the first thing they teach you at the Spanish football academy?

How TAPAS the ball

What is a cow's favourite stadium in Spain?

The MOO camp

Who is the most bad-mannered player in La Liga?

RUDE Bellingham

What do you get if you cross a top Spanish defender with a WWE wrestler?

Sergio SLAM-os

QUICK QUIZ

CAN YOU NAME THE THREE TEAMS WHO HAVE WON THE PREMIER LEAGUE, BUT ONLY WON IT ONCE?

    13 = MANCHESTER UNITED
    7 = MANCHESTER CITY
    5 = CHELSEA
    3 = ARSENAL
    1 = _____, _____ AND _____ ?

Why does Jesus score so many headers?

He's good at getting onto a CROSS

What do Ghosts practise in training?

DEAD ball situations!

Jokey Book
FOOTBALL EDITION

BREAKING NEWS!!

The Swedish national team have appointed the founder of **IKEA** as their new manager...

...he says his defence will play as a **FLAT-PACK** four!

Best EVER premiership XI

Ashley Cole
Arsenal
Chelsea

Ryan Giggs
Manchester United

Virgil Van Dijk
Southampton
Liverpool

Eric Cantona
Leeds
Manchester United

Peter Schmeichel
Manchester United
Manchester City
Aston Villa

Steven Gerrard
Liverpool

Paul Scholes
Manchester United

Thierry Henry
Arsenal

Vincent Kompany
Manchester City

Kyle Walker
Spurs
Manchester City

Mo Salah
Chelsea
Liverpool

What's yours??

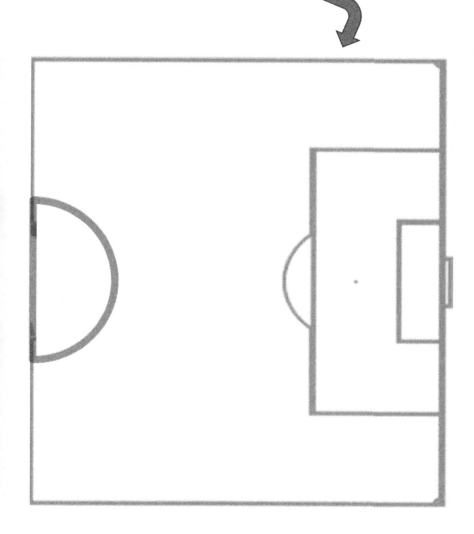

WHO IS A BETTER DIVER: NEYMAR OR A DOLPHIN?

During the 2018 World Cup in Russia, Neymar spent a total of 14 minutes rolling on the floor across Brazil's 5 matches, averaging 3.6 rolls (or revolutions) per dive, and twice maxing out at a whopping five rolls!

Although dolphins can perform front flips, never has a dolphin been recorded as performing more than one flip (or revolution), however they can leap up to 15 feet straight out of the water, so although Neymar wins in terms of activity, the dolphin clearly wins in terms of height.

WINNER: DRAW

Why are magicians so good at football?

They always get Hat-Tricks

Why do football fans in Central America always get wet?

Because of the Mexican waves!

QUESTION: When you were little, didn't you think offside was another name for a throw-in?

Because, like, the ball goes **OFF** the **SIDE** of the pitch...

...or was that just me?

NOT SO... QUICK QUIZ

THIS IS A TOUGH ONE, YOU MIGHT WANT TO GET YOUR DAD, OR EVEN YOUR GRANDAD TO HELP YOU... I BET EVEN THEY CANNOT GET THEM ALL... USE THE OPPOSITE PAGE TO KEEP TRACK

AS OF THE START OF THE 23/24 PREMIER LEAGUE SEASON THERE ARE A TOTAL OF 31 (THIRTY-ONE) TEAMS WHO HAVE PREVIOUSLY BEEN IN THE PREMIERSHIP, BUT CURRENTLY ARE <u>NOT</u>...

HOW MANY CAN YOU GET?

25-30 = BALLON D'OR WINNER
20-25 = WORLD CLASS
15-20 = PREMIER LEAGUE HALL OF FAMER
10-15 = FOOTBALL LEAGUE STALWART
5-10 = NON-LEAGUE SEMI-PRO
1-5 = SUNDAY LEAGUE PLAYER
0   EGG CHASER (RUGBY FAN)

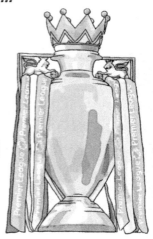

1. _____ ____
2. _____ _____
3. ___
4. _____ _____
5. _____
6. _____ ____
7. _____ ____
8. _____ _____
9. _____
10. _____ _____
11. _____
12. _____ ____
13. _____ ____
14. _____ _____
15. _____ _____
16. _____
17. _____
18. _____ _____
19. _____ ____
20. _____
21. _____ ____
22. ____ _____ _____
23. _____
24. _____ _____
25. _____
26. _____ ____
27. ____ ____
28. _____
29. _____ ____
30. _____ ____
31. _____ ____

Jokey Book
Football Edition

Where do clowns stay on a football pitch?

In the centre circus!

How does Santa set up his team?

4-5-1 (Christmas tree formation!)

Why does Andre Onana's mum hate laundry day?

He never has clean sheets!

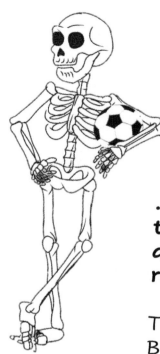

Why do skeleton strikers always score great goals?

They've perfected the ra-BONE-a...

...Unfortunately though, skeleton defenders are rubbish...

They keep scoring BONE goals

QUESTION:

Is it possible to play a square pass in the centre circle?

JOKEY BOOK

FOOTBALL EDITION

GERMANY: DEUTSCHLAND
Bundesliga

Which German team never lies?

Bayern TRUE-nic

Football is a simple game. Twenty-Two men chase a ball for 90 minutes and at the end, the Germans always win.

Quote by Gary Lineker

Who finishes bottom of the Bundesliga?

The WURST team

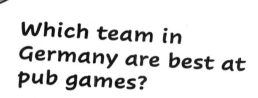

Which team in Germany are best at pub games?

Borussia DARTS-mund

Which German striker never gets hungry?

Tomas FULLER

QUICK QUIZ

THE WORLD RECORD SCORE FOR A FOOTBALL MATCH WAS 149-0!

THE AMAZING RESULT OCCURRED IN A MADAGASCAN LEAGUE PLAYOFF BETWEEN AS ADEMA AND L'EMYRNE.

DO YOU KNOW WHAT THE CIRCUMSTANCES WERE THAT LEAD TO THIS? AND HOW AS ADEMA CAME TO SCORE SUCH A HUGE NUMBER OF GOALS (1.6 GOALS PER MINUTE)

What does a manager do when the pitch gets water-logged?

Sends on his subs

What game do Barcelona play on the team bus?

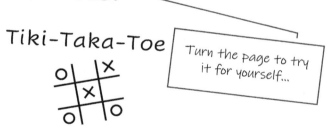

Tiki-Taka-Toe

Turn the page to try it for yourself...

What does a football agent do when he gets too hot?

Opens the transfer window!

FOOTBALL TIKI-TAKA-TOE

JUST LIKE THE CLASSIC TIC-TAC-TOE GAME (NOUGHTS AND CROSSES), BUT IN ORDER TO GAIN A SQUARE, YOU MUST NAME A PLAYER THAT HAS PLAYED FOR BOTH TEAMS ON THAT INTERSECTION...

... CHECK OUT THE EXAMPLE BELOW AND THEN PLAY ON THE NEXT PAGE...

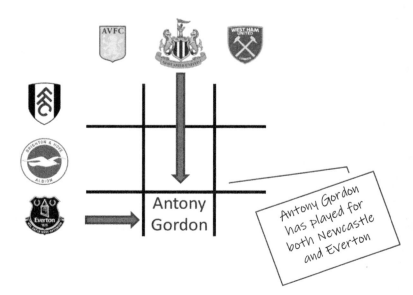

Antony Gordon has played for both Newcastle and Everton

FOOTBALL TIKI-TAKA-TOE

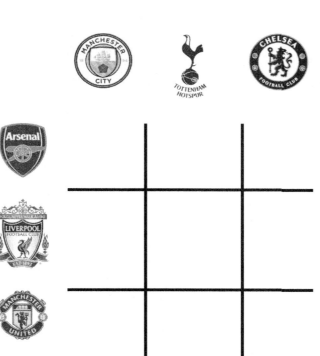

SEE PAGE 63 FOR ONE POSSIBLE SOLUTION

WHO'S GOT BETTER HAIR: GREALISH OR A LION?

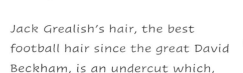

Jack Grealish's hair, the best football hair since the great David Beckham, is an undercut which, together with his Alice band, makes way for the stunning slicked back look that's got England fans swooning, but has limited functionality.

In the animal world, most male lions grow impressive manes the older they get. These manes can grow up to 16cm long and are a sign of dominance, fitness and strength. The Longer, thicker and darker a mane is, the more attractive the lion is to females.

So, if hair is a sign of strength, I guess it all boils down to who would win in a fight!

WINNER: LION

QUICK QUIZ

WHO IS THE ONLY PLAYER TO HAVE WON THE PREMIER LEAGUE IN BACK-TO-BACK SEASONS BUT WITH TWO DIFFERENT CLUBS?

------ ----- ?

COMING SOON...

COMING SOON...

QUICK QUIZ ANSWERS?

PAGE ??: THE END

PAGE ??: YOU ABSOLUTE LEGEND. NEVER GIVE UP!!

PAGE ??: IF YOU ARE STILL READING DOWN THIS FAR YOU'RE GENUINELY NOT RIGHT

PAGE ??: THIS IS GETTING SILLY

PAGE ??: SERIOUSLY?

PAGE ??: WHY ARE YOU STILL READING THIS? THE ANSWERS ARE ON THE NEXT PAGE

PAGE ??: WELL...GO ON THEN

PAGE ??: NAH, ONLY JOKING. THE ANSWERS ARE ON THE NEXT PAGE...

PAGE ??: NO, SERIOUSLY! FORGET IT

PAGE ??: WE ARE NOT GIVING YOU THE ANSWERS

PAGE ?: STOP CHEATING

QUICK QUIZ ANSWERS:

PAGE 2: ENGLAND IN 1966, AND SPAIN IN 2010

PAGE 13: FRANCE AND ITALY [EUROPEAN CHAMPIONSHIP FINAL 2000, WORLD CUP FINAL 2006]

PAGE 32: GERMANY [MENS WORLD CUP WINNERS 1954, 1974, 1990, 2006 WOMENS WORLD CUP WINNERS 2003, 2007]
SPAIN [MENS WORLD CUP WINNERS 2010
WOMENS WORLD CUP WINNERS 2023]

PAGE 40: BLACKBURN ROVERS 1995, LEICESTER CITY 2016, LIVERPOOL 2020

PAGE 52: L'EMYRNE PLANNED TO LOSE AS A PROTEST AGAINST REFEREEING DECISIONS IN A PREVIOUS GAME. - ALL 149 GOALS WERE OWN GOALS!!

PAGE 57: N'GOLO KANTE [LEICESTER CITY 15/16 AND CHELSEA 16/17]

NOT SO... QUICK QUIZ ANSWERS:

1. NORWICH CITY
2. BLACKBURN ROVERS
3. QPR
4. SHEFFIELD WEDNESDAY
5. WIMBLEDON
6. COVENTRY CITY
7. IPSWICH TOWN
8. LEEDS UNITED
9. SOUTHAMPTON
10. OLDHAM ATHLETIC
11. MIDDLESBROUGH
12. SWINDON TOWN
13. LEICESTER CITY
14. BOLTON WANDERERS
15. DERBY COUNTY
16. SUNDERLAND
17. BARNSLEY
18. CHARLTON ATHLETIC
19. BRADFORD CITY
20. WATFORD
21. BIRMINGHAM CITY
22. WEST BROMWICH ALBION
23. PORTSMOUTH
24. WIGAN ATHLETIC
25. READING
26. STOKE CITY
27. HULL CITY
28. BLACKPOOL
29. SWANSEA CITY
30. CARDIFF CITY
31. HUDDERSFIELD TOWN

FOOTBALL TIKI-TAKA-TOE

Carlos Tevez	Michael Carrick	Mason Mount
James Milner	Robbie Keane	Mo Salah
Gabriel Jesus	William Gallas	Kai Havertz

Buy
JOKEY BOOKS:

Follow:

SEND US A JOKE!!

Do you have a really funny joke, on any subject, not just football?

We want to hear it.

Send it to: email@glasdek.co.uk with 'JOKE' in the subject header.

If we like it, we might include it in a future edition of Jokey Book, so don't forget to include your name and age

Acknowledgements:

Logobyb.co.uk
 @logobyb2

Mikey Smith

1001fonts.com
Larabiefonts.com

Printed in Great Britain
by Amazon